People in the
Rain Forest

Saviour Pirotta

WAYLAND

Deep in the
Rain Forest

PEOPLE in the Rain Forest   RIVERS in the Rain Forest
PREDATORS in the Rain Forest   TREES AND PLANTS in the Rain Forest

Cover picture: Cofan Indians in the Amazon rain forest
in Ecuador, dressed for a special festival.

Title page: A ten-year-old boy outside his house in the
Amazon. His house has walls made of sticks and mud.

Contents page: A hunter in the rain forests
of Madagascar.

Editor: Polly Goodman
Designer: Tim Mayer
Consultant: Anne Marley, Principal Librarian,
Children and Schools Library Service, Hants.

First published in 1998 by
Wayland Publishers Ltd
61 Western Road, Hove
East Sussex BN3 1JD, England

Find Wayland on the Internet at
http://www.wayland.co.uk

British Library Cataloguing in Publication Data
Pirotta, Saviour, 1958–
    People in the rain forest.
    – (Deep in the rain forest)
    1. Rain forest – Juvenile literature
    2. Human ecology – Juvenile literature
    I. Title
    581.7'34

ISBN 0 7502 2197 6

Printed and bound by Eurografica, Italy

Contents

Rain Forests around the World

Rain forests are thick forests in parts of the world where there is lots of rain. Most of them are near the Equator, an imaginary line that runs around the centre of the earth. The biggest rain forest is the Amazon, in South America.

◀ A rainforest family's tree house in Sri Lanka.

▼ Asmat people in Indonesia.

EQUATOR

◀ This boy lives on the island of Madagascar.

■ The green areas on the map show rain forests.

People have lived in rain forests for thousands of years. They live in harmony with the forest around them, scattered in small villages which are built on cleared land.

◀ Cofan Indians in the Amazon rain forest in Ecuador, dressed for a special occasion

▼ This Jivaro man lives in Peru.

▲ Kayapo people live in the Amazon rain forest in Brazil.

Rainforest Homes

Rainforest people build their homes using materials they can find nearby. The Yanomani people live in the Amazon. They build enormous huts called *malocas*. Many families share one *maloca*.

▲ Hammocks are cool and comfortable to sleep in.

Yanomani people live together like one big family. They help each other with jobs like cooking and growing food. Every family in the *maloca* has its own space, where they can sleep and keep their belongings.

◀ The roof of the maloca is made from the leaves of palm trees.

Tree and stilt houses

Some rainforest people live in tree houses.
They climb up to them using steps made
from the branches of trees.

Many rainforest houses are built on stilts.
They keep dry when the ground is flooded.

▲ Houses built on stilts in Papua New Guinea.

 8

▼ This tree house in Sri Lanka protects people from elephants.

Hunting and Farming

Rainforest people are experts at hunting and gathering food. Some hunt with spears, or bows and arrows. Others blow poisoned darts through long, bamboo pipes. Many people fish from dugout canoes on the rivers.

▲ A boy in Papua New Guinea using a bow and arrow to shoot fish.

Many different animals are hunted for food. Monkeys, birds, tortoises and wild pigs are favourites. Cane rats, caterpillars and snails can be tasty, too.

At the end of the day, the hunters bring home their catch to roast on the fire.

▲ A hunter in Madagascar using a sharp spear.

Farming

▼ A girl peeling a manioc root in the Amazon.

Rainforest people grow only what they need in the rain forest, without causing damage. They clear small patches of land near their homes, and grow crops such as manioc, maize, sweet potatoes, bananas and nuts.

Since the soil is poor, the plot is changed every two years. Then the old farmland becomes rain forest again.

▼ Kayapo women carry home a harvest of maize.

Food and Medicine

Rainforest people hunt or grow most of the food they eat. Manioc is a vegetable that is eaten by most rainforest people. It can be eaten in many different ways.

People grate and pound manioc before roasting it. Manioc flour can be made into bread or pancakes.

▼ Manioc pancakes and meat parcels wrapped in banana leaves cooking on a huge frying pan.

◀ A Kayapo man in Brazil with a tortoise ready to be cooked.

Sometimes people cook piracuru, which is a giant fish that lives in the Amazon. Its tongue is so hard that it can be used to grate manioc. Tortoise and wild pigs are very popular too. Their meat is wrapped in banana leaves and smoked over a slow fire.

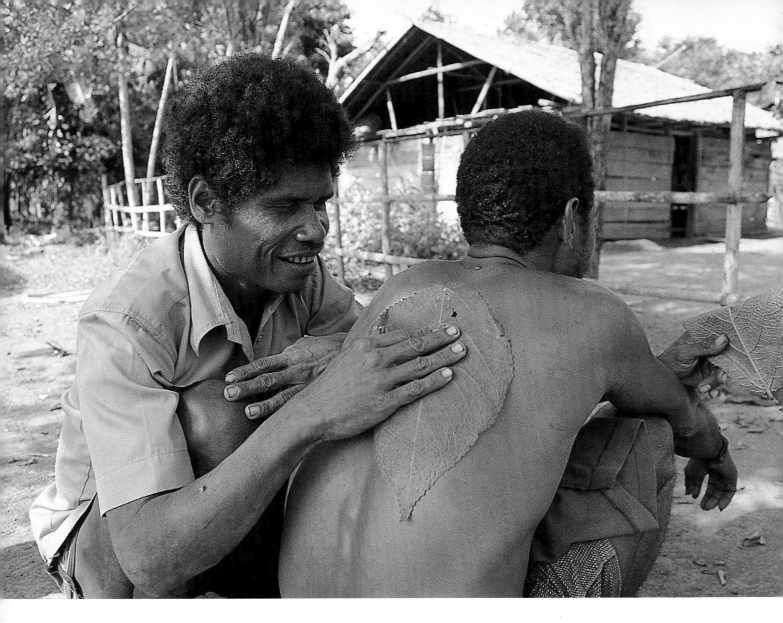

▲ A Ceram man in Indonesia using a leaf called a 'devil's leaf' to treat his friend's rheumatism.

Medicines

Many natural medicines grow in the rain forests. Rainforest people know more about them than anyone else in the world. The medicine man's herbs can cure anything from upset stomachs to deadly snake bites.

Some rainforest people collect the medical plants and sell them on market stalls. The plants and knowledge about them are very valuable to people all over the world. The medicines often reach many different countries.

◀ A Dayak woman in Borneo picks the leaves of a plant called lia lamut. They cure skin diseases and act as painkillers.

Religion and Festivals

Rainforest people have one of the oldest religions in the world. They believe that the world around them is full of spirits, which live in the water, the hills and the streams.

The shaman is the most important person in the village. He knows how to contact the spirits.

◀ A shaman with a crown of feathers and string of birds that have died. They show that he can contact the spirit world.

▲ These Asmat men in Indonesia are honouring
a sago tree with a special ceremony.

The spirits look after people by making sure
the crops ripen and the hunting is good. So the
people take care of the forest around them to
keep the spirits happy.

▲ The Kayapo people in the Amazon have painted their faces and bodies to do this special dance.

Festivals

Sometimes rainforest people have festivals to honour the spirits, or to ask for their help. Hunters often dance so they will catch better prey. They paint patterns on their faces and bodies.

◀ Hudoq people in Indonesia at their rice-planting festival.

The Hudoq people in Indonesia do a special dance at rice-planting time, to ask the spirits for a good rice crop. They wear huge masks and robes made of banana leaves.

▼ Cofan people in Ecuador wearing costumes for a special festival.

People in Danger

Many rainforest people have lost their homes and their hunting grounds because the rain forest is being destroyed. Big logging and mining companies are chopping down all the trees.

▼ A tin mine in the Amazon.

This family have been ▶
made homeless because
a logging company has
taken away their land.

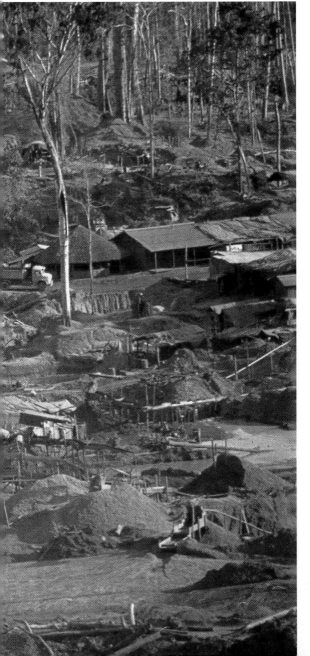

The trees are sold to countries like
Britain and the USA, to make furniture.

More forest is destroyed as people from
the cities and large companies burn vast
areas of forest for houses and farmland.

Diseases

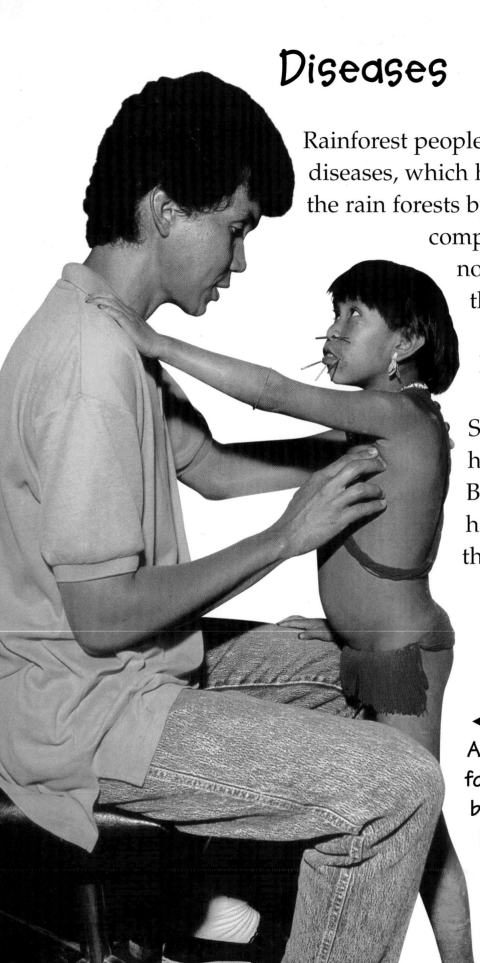

Rainforest people are suffering from new diseases, which have been brought to the rain forests by mining and logging companies. The people do not know how to cure them, so doctors from outside the rain forests have to help.

Some rainforest people have begun to eat sugar. But since many do not have toothpaste as well, the sugar rots their teeth.

◀ A **doctor** in the Amazon checks a child for an eye disease, brought to the area by goldminers.

▲ Rainforest people being taken to work in the mines.

As rainforest people lose their hunting grounds, they have to find other work. Many people work in the mines, for very low wages.

The traditional rainforest way of life is disappearing. If this happens, the valuable knowledge of rainforest peoples will be lost forever.

▲ Dayak people in Borneo block a road to stop logging trucks destroying their land.

Fighting back

Some rainforest people are fighting back. They are protesting to their government to stop people destroying the rain forest.

Some, like the Yakuna group in Colombia, have won their lands back. They can make sure that the rain forest is saved forever.

Finding out more

We can learn a lot from rainforest people. Many tourists can now visit the rain forests. They can learn about the forests from the people and find out about their struggles.

If more outsiders know about the people of the rain forests, they have a better chance of survival. You can help by finding out as much as you can.

▼ This American boy is being taught how to play some pipes by a rainforest chief in Peru.

Face Painting

Before a celebration, many rainforest people paint their faces with colourful patterns. Copy one of the patterns shown opposite, or design your own rainforest pattern.

YOU WILL NEED:

● A friend to be your model.

● Water-based face paints: red, yellow and purple. You can get these in a theatre or specialist make-up suppliers.

● Brushes: 1 thin (for drawing fine lines) 1 thick (for drawing thicker lines).

● Sponges: for filling in big areas.

● A t-shirt: make sure it's OK to get paint on it.

● An adult: don't start face painting without an adult there to help.

HANDY HINTS

● Start with simple patterns first. People's skin is quite rubbery and hard to draw on. It's best to get used to it before you do a complicated design.

● If you want to try some more patterns, you could find them in photographic books about the rain forest.

WARNING!

Brushes are sometimes thin and sharp. Be VERY CAREFUL if you're painting someone else's face, especially if you're painting near their eyes.

1. This man is from the Tara Huli people in Papua New Guinea. Use a brush to draw the outline of this pattern first. Then colour it in using a sponge.

2. This Jivaro man is from the Amazon rain forest in Peru. Use a thin brush to copy this pattern.

3. This pattern is on a Yanomani girl in Brazil. Start this pattern from the bottom of one cheek. Copy it up the side of the face and over the forehead to the bottom of the other cheek.

29

Further Information

Books to read

Look Who Lives in the Rain Forest by Alan Baker (MacDonald Young Books, 1998)

People and Places in Peril: Rainforests by Sara Oldfield (Cherrytree Books, 1995)

Peoples Under Threat: Rainforest Amerindians by Anna Lewington (Wayland, 1995)

What do we know about Amazonian Indians by Anna Lewington (MacDonald Young Books, 1993)

World of the Rain Forest by Rosie McCormick (TwoCan, 1997)

Worldwise: Rainforest by Penny Clarke (Watts, 1996)

CD Rom

Exploring Land Habitats (Wayland, 1997)

Audio tape

Environmental Sounds: Tropical Jungle (The Nature Company, Tel: 001 510 644 1337) – recordings from the Amazon, including a rainstorm passing overhead, a jaguar's roar and spider monkey's chatter.

Useful addresses

All these groups provide material on rain forests for schools:

Friends of the Earth (UK)
26-28 Underwood Street, London N1 7QJ
Tel: 0171 490 1555
Internet: www. for.co.uk/

Living Earth Foundation
4 Great James Street
London WC1N 3DA
Tel: 0171 242 3816
Internet: http://www.gn.apc.org/Living Earth

Reforest The Earth
42–46 Bethel Street,
Norwich NR2 1NR
Tel: 01603 611953

Worldwide Fund for Nature
Panda House
Wayside Park
Cattleshall Lane
Godalming GU7 1XR
Tel: 01608 676691
Internet: http://www.wwf-uk.org

Picture acknowledgements
Bruce Coleman (Alain Compost) 4 (top), 5 (left), (Luiz Claudio Marigo) 14, (Alain Compost) 16, 19, 21 (top); Sue Cunningham Photographic Library *Title page*, 6, 13, 20, 23, 25; Getty Images Limited (Art Wolfe) 29 (middle); Impact (Caroline Penn) 8; NHPA (Daniel Heuclin) *Contents page*, 4 (bottom), (Karl Switak) 10, (Daniel Heuclin) 11, 15; Oxford Scientific Films (Aldo Brando) 18; Edward Parker 12; Planet Earth Pictures (Pete Oxford) *Cover*, 5 (top), 21 (bottom); South American Pictures (Index Editora) 29 (bottom); Still Pictures (Mark Edwards) 5 (right), 7, 9, (Nigel Dickinson) 17, (Mark Edwards) 22, 24, (Nigel Dickinson) 26, (Michael Doolittle) 26 and 27; Trip 29 (top).
Border and folio artwork: Kate Davenport. Map pages 4–5 and artwork page 6: Peter Bull.

Topic Web and Notes

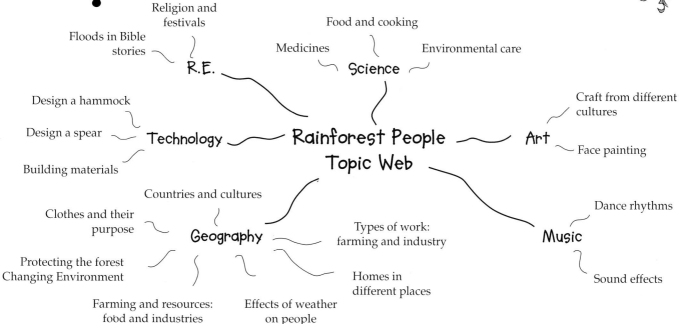

Religion and festivals

Floods in Bible stories

R.E.

Medicines

Food and cooking

Science

Environmental care

Design a hammock

Design a spear

Technology

Building materials

Craft from different cultures

Rainforest People Topic Web

Art

Face painting

Countries and cultures

Clothes and their purpose

Geography

Protecting the forest Changing Environment

Types of work: farming and industry

Dance rhythms

Music

Homes in different places

Sound effects

Farming and resources: food and industries

Effects of weather on people

GEOGRAPHY
• To help children understand there are different nationalities and indigenous groups living in the rain forests, ask them to find pictures of people from three different countries in the book. Compare their clothes and houses.

• Ask the children to imagine it is always hot. Would they wear the same clothes as they are now?

• Make up a story about a city child who heard a rainforest sound at night e.g. the roar of a tiger. Now make up a different story about a rainforest child who hears a sound from the city e.g. the squealing of car tyres. Compare their reactions.

• Ask the children to compare a maloca or a treehouse to their own home (see page 6–9). What are the differences? Discuss what would happen if you put a maloca in your neighbourhood and your own house in the rain forest.

TECHNOLOGY
• Design a spear or a bow and arrow (look at pages 10–11). Draw plans on paper, and discuss the materials you would need. Which materials would work best? Can they be found in the forest?

SCIENCE
• Collect various foods that come from the rain forest e.g. bananas, Brazil nuts, star fruit. Discuss how living on them would affect your health. Are they better for you than some popular foods in the developed world?

• List the dangers of living in the rain forest. If you were a medicine man or woman, what types of illnesses would you need medicines for?

R.E
• Compare the religion and festivals in the rain forest to a different major world religion. You could compare the Hudoq rice-planting festival on page 21 to Harvest festival or Thanksgiving.

MUSIC
• Compare the sounds found in the rain forest to those in the city. Which sounds do you prefer?

DANCE/DRAMA
• Make up a dance, thanking the spirits of the forest for the harvest. You could include this in your harvest festival celebrations.

Glossary

Amazon A region or rain forest in South America around the Amazon river.

Crops Plants that are grown for food, including wheat, corn and rice.

Logging Cutting down trees so that the wood can be sold.

Maize A cereal crop, with large ears of yellow seeds growing on tall stalks.

Maloca A type of house used by the Yanomani people, in Brazil.

Manioc A root vegetable that grows under the ground.

Minerals Substances like oil, coal or metal that mining companies dig from the ground.

Painkillers Medicines that help reduce pain.

Protesting Arguing strongly.

Rheumatism A disease causing pain and stiffness around the joints.

Ripen Become ready to be harvested, or eaten.

Shaman A special person in the rain forests who is able to contact the spirits.

Spirits Invisible forces.

Index

Page numbers in **bold** show there is a picture on the page as well as information.